Big Frog Track

By Carmel Reilly

Mack and Liz will walk
on Big Frog Track.

Big Frog Track has
a little shack.

Liz got her hat
and a red back-pack.

Liz put a jacket
in her back-pack.

Liz packed some snacks.

She packed the snacks
into her back-pack.

Mack got his black back-pack.

Mack put snacks and a hat in his back-pack.

snacks

Mack and Liz looked at a map of Big Frog Track.

"We can walk to the shack and back," said Liz.

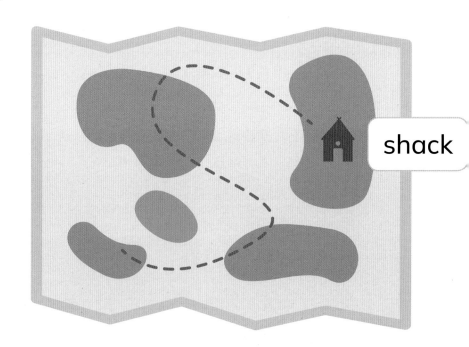

shack

Mack and Liz walked
to the shack.

They had a snack
and a drink.

It got cold.

Liz put on her jacket.

Then, Mack and Liz walked back on the track.

It was a big day!

CHECKING FOR MEANING

1. What colour is Mack's back-pack? *(Literal)*

2. Who packed the snacks? *(Literal)*

3. What time of day do you think Mack and Liz walked to the shack? *(Inferential)*

EXTENDING VOCABULARY

shack	What does the word *shack* mean? What is another word with a similar meaning? Where might you find a shack?
back-pack	Look at the word *back-pack*. Which two smaller words make up this word?
It's	Look at the word *It's*. What two words is this word short for? What other contractions do you know?

MOVING BEYOND THE TEXT

1. Where might you find a track?

2. How are tracks different from roads?

3. What do you need to pack if you are going on a hike?

4. What are some things you can do to stay safe when you are hiking?

SPEED SOUNDS

at	an	ap	et	og	ug

ell	ack	ash	ing

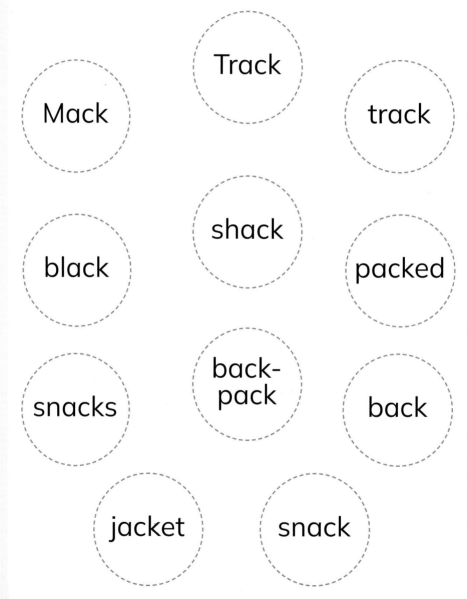

Track

Mack

track

shack

black

packed

snacks

back-
pack

back

jacket

snack